COOKBOOK

TOBLERONE
▲ OF SWITZERLAND ▲

COOKBOOK
40 FABULOUS BAKING TREATS

Photography by Maja Smend

KYLE BOOKS

An Hachette UK Company
www.hachette.co.uk

First published in Great Britain in 2020 by
Kyle Books, an imprint of Kyle Cathie Ltd
Carmelite House
50 Victoria Embankment
London EC4Y 0DZ
www.kylebooks.co.uk

This edition published in 2020

ISBN: 978 0 85783 908 4

Toblerone® is a brand of Mondelez international Company
Group and is used under licence

Distributed in the US by Hachette Book Group, 1290 Avenue of
the Americas, 4th and 5th Floors, New York, NY 10104

Distributed in Canada by Canadian Manda Group, 664 Annette
St., Toronto, Ontario, Canada M6S 2C8

Editorial Director: Judith Hannam
Publisher: Joanna Copestick
Editor: Isabel Gonzalez-Prendergast
Recipe creation & food styling: Lottie Covell
Photography: Maja Smend
Design: Paul Palmer-Edwards
Props styling: Olivia Wardle
Production: Katherine Hockley

Printed and bound in China

10 9 8 7 6 5 4 3 2 1

CONTENTS

INTRODUCTION

In 1908, celebrated Swiss chocolatier Theodor Tobler and his cousin Emil Baumann were on a trip to France when they discovered torrone: a white nougat made from almonds, honey, and sugar. Knowing they had found something special, the pair combined their Tobler's Swiss milk chocolate with this delicious confection to create the first ever TOBLERONE.

Confectionery was in Theodor's blood. His father, Jean, a confectioner and pastry chef, opened Confiserie Spéciale in 1868 in the Länggass quarter of Bern, Switzerland. Running the business with his wife Adelina, Theodor's mother, they sold caramels, candied fruit, Easter eggs and pralines, although at the time they did not produce their own chocolate. By the time Theodor and his brother joined the family business, it was time to expand. The family chocolate factory opened in 1899, and Tobler chocolate quickly became renowned.

With the invention of TOBLERONE, the business grew rapidly. Now, more than a century later, despite being sold in over 120 countries worldwide, every single TOBLERONE is still lovingly made in one factory in Bern, with the same level of quality and passion as the first one. Its distinctive shape, classic packaging and memorable logo has made TOBLERONE the world's most iconic chocolate: a progressive, triangular treat in a sea of squares and bars. The well-known

TOBLERONE lettering and branding make it instantly recognizable, but did you know there's a hidden image in our iconic Matterhorn logo? Look closely and see if you can spot the bear, the emblem of Bern, scaling the mountain's famous peak.

TOBLERONE has always been associated with gifting and sharing. Its packaging and unusual shape make it the perfect present, while the satisfying way in which each triangular chunk can be snapped off means it is easy and fun to share. TOBLERONE is sold in airports all over the world, making it a favorite gift for travelers returning home.

The recipes in this book take this a step further and provide new ways for you to connect and share with loved ones, capturing all the joy and delicious flavor of Toblerone in new and creative ways. Try our TOBLERONE Trio Brownies (page 30), a tasty way to combine white, dark, and milk chocolate, or indulge in a decadent Blackout TOBLERONE Cake (page 48). Impress your friends and family with a beautifully crafted Milk TOBLERONE, Almond, and Pear Tart (page 90), or treat yourself to an elaborate TOBLERONE Freakshake (page 12). From simple bakes to celebration cakes and spectacular desserts, enjoy all the wonderful ways you can bring this much-loved chocolate into your kitchen.

I

NO-BAKE

ROCKY ROAD

An old favorite, whatever age you are, and perfect if you don't have much time. Keep in a sealed container in your refrigerator, though for best results bring out 30 minutes before serving.

Makes 16 squares, using a 9in square cake tin lined with parchment paper

Prep: 15 minutes
Chill: 4 hours minimum

5½oz unsalted butter
3 tablespoons runny honey
7oz TOBLERONE dark chocolate, plus extra for decorating, chopped
1¾oz raisins

7oz OREO cookies, roughly chopped
3½oz mini marshmallows
5½oz mini TOBLERONE milk chocolate chunks

1. Melt the butter, honey, and dark chocolate in a large saucepan over a gentle heat. Remove from the heat and stir in the raisins, OREO cookies, and half of the marshmallows until completely coated in the chocolate. Stir in half the chocolate chunks and pour into the prepared tin. Flatten with the back of a spoon and sprinkle over the remaining chopped dark chocolate, marshmallows, and mini chocolate chunks.

2. Cover with plastic wrap and chill in the refrigerator for at least 4 hours until set or keep in the refrigerator until ready to serve. Cut into 16 squares and store in an airtight container for 4–5 days in the refrigerator.

Tip: Try mixing up the cookies with your favorites – butter or ginger cookies both work well.

TOBLERONE FREAKSHAKE

A fun and decadent twist on a classic, topped with lashings of whipped cream! This recipe serves one but can easily be doubled, tripled, or quadrupled...

Serves 1

Prep: 10 minutes

2 tablespoons Rich Chocolate Sauce (see page 27) or ready-made chocolate sauce

1 banana, peeled and frozen
3½oz No-churn TOBLERONE Caramel Ice Cream (see page 27) or 3½oz vanilla ice cream and 1¾oz TOBLERONE milk chocolate, roughly chopped
3½fl oz whole milk

squirty cream
2 fresh cherries
Handful of mini TOBLERONE milk chocolate chunks
1 small piece of Millionaire's Shortbread (see page 51)
rainbow sprinkles

1. If using the rich chocolate sauce, warm through in a small saucepan over a gentle heat, then drizzle down the sides of a large sundae glass (approx 14fl oz). Put in the freezer for 15 minutes to set.

2. Put the banana, ice cream, and milk in a powerful blender and blitz until smooth. Pour into the chilled glass.

3. Top with squirty cream, cherries, chocolate chunks, and a small millionaire shortbread, brownie, or cake of your choice (see Tip). Shake over rainbow sprinkles and enjoy straight away with a spoon.

Tip: Try adding your favorite berries and swapping chocolate sauce for salted caramel. Experiment with different toppings, such as the TOBLERONE and Berry Blondies (see page 32) or TOBLERONE Crispy Cakes (see page 19).

CHOCOLATE BARK

This looks incredibly impressive but couldn't be easier to make.
It really won't take you longer than 20 minutes from start to finish.

Serves 10, using an 8 x 12in baking sheet lined with parchment paper

Prep: 20 minutes
Chill: 2 hours minimum

10½oz TOBLERONE dark chocolate
5½oz TOBLERONE white chocolate
1oz toasted flaked almonds

handful mini TOBLERONE milk chocolate chunks

1. Melt the dark and white chocolate in two separate heatproof bowls set over two saucepans of barely simmering water, making sure the bowls don't touch the water. Stir until smooth.

2. Pour the melted dark chocolate over the prepared baking sheet. Then drizzle or carefully spoon the melted white chocolate on top. Use a skewer to marble in the white chocolate. When you are happy with the pattern, sprinkle over the flaked almonds and mini chocolate chunks. Transfer to the refrigerator to set for at least 2 hours.

3. Break the chocolate bark into pieces to serve, and store in an airtight container in the refrigerator for 1-2 weeks.

Tip: Swap the toppings with your favorite fruit and nut combinations, try freeze-dried raspberries and different chopped nuts such as hazelnuts or chopped Brazil nuts. You can also experiment with different flavors of chocolate but remember you need different tones of chocolate to make the marbled effect.

CHOCOLATE TRUFFLES

If you are looking for an easy-to-make edible gift or something to accompany a coffee, these are perfect. As they're made with fresh cream, they should be stored in the refrigerator.

Makes 32

Prep: 50 minutes
Chill: 5½ hours minimum

1¾oz unsalted butter
1¼ cups (10fl oz) heavy cream
14oz TOBLERONE milk chocolate, roughly chopped
generous pinch of fine sea salt
2 tablespoons Amaretto or your

favorite liqueur (optional)
1¾oz almonds, toasted and finely chopped
7oz TOBLERONE dark chocolate, roughly chopped

1. Melt the butter and cream in a medium saucepan over a gentle heat, stirring occasionally. Put the chocolate and salt in a medium mixing bowl and pour over the hot cream mixture. Stir with a spatula until the chocolate has melted and you have a thick chocolate sauce. Stir in the Amaretto, if using, then leave the bowl to cool for 5 minutes before putting in the refrigerator. Chill, covered, for 5 hours or overnight if possible.

2. Use a teaspoon or melon baller to scoop out balls of the chilled chocolate mixture, then shape in your hands to form smooth balls. Put half the truffles on a plate and chill in the freezer for 30 minutes. Coat the other half in the chopped almonds and set aside.

3. Melt the dark chocolate in a small, heatproof bowl set over a saucepan of barely simmering water, making sure the bowl doesn't touch the water. Stir until smooth and let cool a little.

4. Dip the chilled truffles in the melted chocolate. Sit on a plate and transfer to the refrigerator to chill until set, about 2–3 hours. Store all the truffles in an airtight container in the refrigerator for up to a week. Remove from the refrigerator an hour before serving so they aren't too cold.

Tip: Swap the almonds for your favorite nut, hazelnuts or pistachios work well.

TOBLERONE CRISPY CAKES

Crispy cakes are perfect party food, loved by children and adults alike. TOBLERONE chocolate makes them all the more delicious! Once they've been chilled you can store them in a sealed container at room temperature and they will last a week.

Makes 25 small squares, using a 9in square cake tin lined with parchment paper

Prep: 20 minutes
Chill: 3 hours

5½oz marshmallows, preferably large
5½oz unsalted butter
3½oz TOBLERONE dark chocolate
7oz puffed wheat, such as Rice Krispies

10½oz TOBLERONE milk chocolate

1. Melt the marshmallows, butter, and dark chocolate in a large, heavy-based saucepan over low heat. Stir regularly until fully combined. Mix in the puffed wheat, then spoon the mixture into the prepared tin. Flatten with the back of a spoon to form a compact and even layer. Chill in the refrigerator for 1 hour.

2. Melt the milk chocolate in a heatproof bowl set over a saucepan of barely simmering water, making sure the bowl doesn't touch the water. Pour evenly over the chilled cake and smooth with the back of a spoon. Cover the pan with plastic wrap and return to the refrigerator for at least 2 hours to set completely.

3. Once set, cut into squares and store in an airtight container for 1 week.

CHOCOLATE POTS

Creamy and velvety in texture, these little pots will sit happily in your refrigerator for 2-3 days. The Cointreau cuts through the rich chocolate and is perfect if you are serving guests for a special dinner but not absolutely necessary. You can leave it out if you prefer, or use a different liquor.

Makes 6, using 6 x 5fl oz ramekins or teacups and saucers

Prep: 20 minutes
Chill: 3-4 hours

5½oz TOBLERONE milk chocolate
5½oz TOBLERONE dark chocolate
9oz mascarpone
5fl oz heavy cream
zest and juice of 3 satsumas
  or clementines
2 tablespoons Cointreau
  (optional)

To serve
raspberries
mini TOBLERONE dark chocolate
  chunks

1. Melt the milk and dark chocolate in a heatproof bowl over a pan of barely simmering water, making sure the bowl doesn't touch the water. Remove from the heat and stir together until smooth. Let cool for 10 minutes.

2. Meanwhile, put the mascarpone, cream, and satsuma zest and juice in a large mixing bowl. Beat together for 3-4 minutes with an electric whisk until creamy and smooth.

3. When the chocolate has cooled, spoon into the bowl with the Cointreau, if using, and whisk into the cream mixture until smooth. Spoon into the ramekins or cups and chill in the refrigerator for 3-4 hours. Serve with raspberries and extra chocolate scattered over the top.

LAYERED COFFEE & TOBLERONE REFRIGERATOR CAKE

If you love coffee, cream, and espresso martinis this is the dessert for you. Your guests will think you have been working for hours in the kitchen, but it is really very simple to make. The Kahlúa is optional but delicious. The cake can be made up to 24 hours in advance but is best served about 5 hours after making.

Serves 14, using a 9in springform cake pan lined with plastic wrap

Prep: 25 minutes
Chill: 3–5 hours

3oz Speculoos cookies
7oz mini TOBLERONE dark chocolate chunks, half roughly chopped
raspberries or cherries, to serve

For the cream filling
2½ cups (20fl oz) heavy cream
9oz mascarpone
3½oz powdered sugar
5½ tablespoons cold coffee, made with 2 tablespoons espresso powder
2fl oz Kahlúa (optional)

1. Put the cream filling ingredients in a large bowl and mix with an electric whisk until the mixture forms soft peaks.

2. Put a layer of cookies over the base of the prepared pan. Top with a quarter of the cream filling and spread evenly. Add another layer of cookies, followed by another one of cream. Sprinkle over the chopped chocolate, then repeat with two more layers of cookies and cream. Top with the reserved chocolate chunks. Loosely cover with plastic wrap and let set in the refrigerator for at least 3 hours, ideally for 5 hours, or until ready to serve.

3. When ready to serve, unclip the pan and carefully move the cake onto a serving plate. Serve straight away with a handful of raspberries or cherries, if liked. It will keep for 2–3 days in the refrigerator.

LIME, WHITE CHOCOLATE, & GINGER CHEESECAKE

Cheesecake is always a winner, but the combination of
white chocolate, lime, and ginger is unbeatable.
Best made no more than 12 hours in advance, it will
nevertheless keep covered in your refrigerator for 2–3 days.

Serves 12, using an 8in loose-based cake tin	9oz ginger biscuits 2¼oz unsalted butter 1lb 7¼oz full-fat cream cheese	5½oz TOBLERONE white chocolate
Prep: 40 minutes, plus chilling	1½ cups (10fl oz) heavy cream 3½oz powdered sugar zest and juice of 4 limes	**To decorate** 5½oz raspberries mini TOBLERONE white chocolate chunks

1. Put the biscuits in a food processor and blitz to a fine crumb. Melt the butter in a medium saucepan, remove from the heat, and stir in the cookies. Press the cookies into the base of the cake pan to form an even, compact layer. Chill in the refrigerator for 30 minutes.

2. Put the cream cheese, cream, powdered sugar, and lime zest and juice in a large mixing bowl and beat with an electric whisk for 4–5 minutes until smooth, thick, and creamy.

3. Melt the white chocolate in a small, heatproof bowl set over a pan of barely simmering water, making sure the bowl doesn't touch the water. Remove from the heat and let cool for 5 minutes. Add to the cream-cheese mixture and use an electric whisk to mix in the melted chocolate. It may seem a little lumpy, but this is normal as the chocolate has nougat in it and the white chocolate may set into the cream. Spoon over the biscuit base and smooth the top using the back of the spoon. Cover with plastic wrap and chill for 4 hours or until ready to serve.

4. To serve, remove the cheesecake from the pan and decorate with the raspberries and mini white chocolate.

NO-CHURN TOBLERONE
CARAMEL ICE CREAM

This ice cream is so easy to make and delicious.
Try mixing up the flavor combinations by adding different
types of TOBLERONE chocolate or a handful of honeycomb.

Serves 8
(makes approx. 5 cups)

Prep: 10 minutes
Freeze: 6 hours minimum

2½ cups (20fl oz) heavy cream
2 x 13oz cans condensed milk
3½oz TOBLERONE white
   chocolate, roughly chopped
3½oz TOBLERONE milk
   chocolate, roughly chopped

3½oz salted caramel sauce
Rich Chocolate Sauce
   (see below), to serve

1. Put the cream, condensed milk, and both types of chocolate in a large mixing bowl and stir together. Pour the mixture into a 2-3 quart sealed container and dollop in the caramel sauce. Swirl through with a fork, then seal and freeze for at least 6 hours.

2. Once ready to serve, scoop into bowls and serve with hot chocolate sauce.

RICH CHOCOLATE SAUCE

This sauce is one to have on hand in the refrigerator. Warm it
through and drizzle over ice cream or other favorite desserts.

Serves 8

Cook: 15 minutes

7oz TOBLERONE dark chocolate
6oz unsalted butter
3½oz superfine sugar

1. Gently melt the chocolate and ⅔ cup water in a heavy-based saucepan over low heat. Stir in the butter and sugar, and slowly melt, stirring occasionally. Simmer for 10-15 minutes until the sauce has thickened a little and is glossy. It will thicken more as it cools. Keep warm until ready to serve.

2. Leave any remaining sauce to cool and pour into an airtight container. Store in the refrigerator for up to 3 weeks.

2

CLASSICS

TOBLERONE TRIO BROWNIES

TOBLERONE chocolate is a brownie's best friend. It works brilliantly in the batter, and adding milk and white chocolate works wonders. This one keeps getting gooier as the week goes on, so don't worry if you still have some left after 3-4 days.

Makes 16–24, using an 8 x 12in rectangular cake pan lined with foil

Prep: 25 minutes
Cook: 45 minutes

9oz unsalted butter
7oz TOBLERONE dark chocolate
7oz TOBLERONE milk chocolate
1 cup (7oz) soft light brown sugar
7oz golden superfine sugar
½ teaspoon fine sea salt

5 extra large eggs
1½ cups (7oz) all-purpose flour
1 teaspoon baking powder
5½oz TOBLERONE white chocolate

1. Preheat the oven to 40°F.

2. Gently melt the butter, dark chocolate, and half the milk chocolate in a heavy-based saucepan over low heat, stirring occasionally, until completely smooth. Pour into a large mixing bowl and use a balloon whisk to add both sugars and the salt. Add the eggs, one at a time, whisking after each addition. Don't worry if the batter splits, it will come back together once the flour is added. Sift in the flour and baking powder and swap the whisk for a spatula. Beat the batter until smooth. Stir in half the white chocolate, then spoon the batter into the prepared tin.

3. Scatter over the remaining chocolate and bake in the middle of the oven for 45–50 minutes. The top should be firm but with some cracks, and the underneath should be set but still squidgy and gooey.

4. Let cool completely in the pan. Chill for 3–4 hours in the refrigerator before slicing into squares. Keep in a sealed container for 1 week.

TOBLERONE & BERRY BLONDIES

If you are a brownie lover, why not try the blonde version,
which is similar in texture but minus the dark chocolate.

**Makes 16, using an 8in square
non-stick cake pan, greased and
lined with a piece of parchment
paper large enough to cover the
base and two sides with at least
a 1in overhang**

5½oz unsalted butter, plus extra
   for greasing
1½ cups (7oz) all-purpose flour
1 teaspoon baking powder
½ teaspoon fine sea salt
2½ tablespoons runny honey
½ cup (3½oz) light brown sugar
2 medium, free-range eggs
1 teaspoon vanilla extract

7oz raspberries
6oz TOBLERONE white
   chocolate, chopped

For the berry compote
2¾oz blackberries
2¾oz blueberries
juice of ½ lemon
1 tablespoon runny honey

1. Preheat the oven to 375°F.

2. To make the berry compote, put all the ingredients in a saucepan and simmer over
   medium heat. Reduce the heat to low and simmer gently for 10 minutes until the fruit
   has broken down and is turning jammy. Remove from the heat and let cool.

3. Add the flour, baking powder, and salt to a large mixing bowl. Melt the butter and
   honey in a small saucepan, then pour into a medium, heatproof bowl. Add the sugar,
   eggs, and vanilla to the melted butter mixture and beat together. Pour over the dry
   ingredients, add most of the raspberries (reserving a large handful for the top), and
   mix together thoroughly using a large spatula. You are looking for a smooth, thick
   batter. Stir in half the chocolate, then pour the batter evenly into the prepared tin.

4. Spoon equal dollops of compote over the batter. Then use a toothpick, skewer, or fine
   knife to swirl the compote lightly into the batter. Top with the remaining raspberries
   and chocolate, then bake on the middle shelf for 26–28 minutes until just set. The
   blondies should still be a little gooey in the middle.

5. Let cool and set in the pan for 2 hours. They will keep for 4–5 days in an airtight
   container in the refrigerator.

Tips: It's easy to swap out the berries for just one variety.

The baked blondies can be frozen. Portion and freeze on a flat tray, then put into small
sandwich bags or wrap in plastic wrap. Grab one the night before to defrost at room
temperature.

CHOCOLATE CUPCAKES

A classic that never gets old. Rich and chocolatey and
very easy to make, they can be frozen, without the icing,
in a sealed container for up to 1 month.

Makes 12, using a 12-hole
cupcake pan lined with cases

Prep: 45 minutes
Cook: 20-22 minutes

5½oz unsalted butter
⅔ cup (5½oz) superfine sugar
3 large eggs, beaten
1 cup (4½oz) self-rising flour
¼ cup (1oz) dark cocoa powder
2¼oz TOBLERONE milk
  chocolate, grated

4 tablespoons whole milk

For the ganache
4¼oz TOBLERONE milk or
  coconut chocolate
7fl oz heavy cream

1. Preheat the oven to 350°F.

2. Put the butter and sugar in a medium mixing bowl, and beat with an electric whisk
   until light and fluffy. Slowly add the beaten egg a little at a time, whisking after each
   addition. Sift in the flour and cocoa powder, and add the chocolate and milk. Use a
   large metal spoon to carefully fold together and divide the mixture evenly between
   the cupcake cases. Bake for 20-22 minutes until risen and a skewer inserted into each
   center comes out clean.

3. Leave the cupcakes to cool on a wire rack. Meanwhile, gently melt the chocolate for
   the ganache in a heatproof bowl set over a saucepan of barely simmering water,
   making sure the bowl doesn't touch the water. Remove from the heat and let cool for
   10 minutes. Then slowly add the cream, whisking constantly until you have a smooth,
   glossy ganache. Cover with plastic wrap and chill in the refrigerator for 1 hour.

4. Spoon the ganache into a disposable piping bag and pipe a simple swirl onto the
   cupcakes or spoon over the top. Transfer to an airtight container and chill until needed.
   Remove from the refrigerator 1 hour before serving. Store in a sealed container in the
   refrigerator for 4-5 days. Bring to room temperature 2 hours before serving.

CHOCOLATE MERINGUE BROWNIE

If brownie wasn't good enough on its own, it just got better.
Crunchy gooey meringue baked on top is a winner and will
definitely impress your friends! Stored in the refrigerator
in a sealed container, it will last 3-4 days.

**Makes 25 squares, using an
8 x 12in rectangular cake pan
lined with parchment paper**

Prep: 40 minutes
Cook: 45 minutes

9oz unsalted butter
9oz TOBLERONE dark chocolate
1¼ cups (9oz) dark muscovado
   sugar
4 extra large eggs
1½ cups (7oz) all-purpose flour
1 teaspoon baking powder
6 mini TOBLERONE dark

chocolate bars, sliced into their
   individual bars, to decorate
cocoa powder, to decorate

For the meringue
4 extra large egg whites
1 cup (8oz) golden superfine
   sugar

1. Preheat the oven to 340°F.

2. Melt the butter and chocolate together in a large saucepan over low heat until smooth.
   Remove from the heat and stir in the sugar. Add one egg at a time, whisking with a
   balloon whisk between additions. Sift in the flour and baking powder, and stir
   together. Pour into the prepared pan and bake for 12 minutes.

3. Meanwhile, tip the egg whites into a large, clean bowl and beat with an electric whisk
   until they form medium-stiff peaks. (You can also do this in the bowl of a stand mixer.)
   Slowly add the sugar, whisking constantly to make a thick, glossy meringue. Spread
   the meringue evenly over the brownie. Return to the oven on a low shelf and bake for
   30 minutes. If the meringue is getting too much color, then cover with foil. The
   brownie should be gooey and the meringue should have formed a crust on top.

4. Let cool completely in the pan. Carefully lift out of the pan, then cut into 25 squares.
   Sprinkle over the chocolate and dust with cocoa powder to serve. Store in an airtight
   container for 4-5 days.

CHOCOLATE GRANOLA FRUIT & NUT BARS

Gooey in the middle but crunchy on the outside, these bars are the perfect snack and very more-ish! They will keep for a week in a sealed container.

Makes 16, using an 8 x 12in rectangular cake pan lined with parchment paper

Prep: 25 minutes
Cook: 25–30 minutes

5½oz unsalted butter
⅔ cup (4½oz) light soft brown sugar
3 tablespoons runny honey
3 cups (10½oz) rolled oats
5½oz mixed dried fruit and nuts (such as cashews, almonds, raisins and cranberries)
3½oz TOBLERONE milk chocolate, roughly chopped
1 teaspoon ground ginger
3½oz TOBLERONE dark chocolate

1. Preheat the oven to 340°F.

2. Melt the butter, sugar, and honey in a medium, heavy-based saucepan over low heat. Remove from the heat and stir in the oats, most of the fruit and nuts, the milk chocolate, and the ground ginger. Mix together thoroughly, then press into the prepared pan. Scatter over the reserved fruit and nuts, and bake for 30–35 minutes until set and a little golden. Remove from the tin, slice into 16 bars, and leave to cool.

3. Melt the dark chocolate in a heatproof bowl set over a saucepan of barely simmering water, making sure the bowl doesn't touch the water. Use a teaspoon to drizzle the melted chocolate over the granola bars. Let set in the refrigerator for 1 hour, then store at room temperature in an airtight container for 1 week.

WHITE TOBLERONE & BLUEBERRY MUFFINS

White chocolate and blueberry are a classic combination,
and they balance each other perfectly. These muffins are
a great addition to a packed lunch, as you can individually
freeze them and defrost as you go.

Makes 12, using a 12-hole muffin pan lined with cases

Prep: 25 minutes
Cook: 30–35 minutes

3½oz unsalted butter, softened
⅜ cup (3½oz) superfine sugar
2 extra large eggs, beaten
150g (5½oz) natural yogurt
1 teaspoon vanilla extract
4 tablespoons whole milk
2 cups (9oz) all-purpose flour

1 teaspoon baking powder
½ teaspoon baking soda
5½oz blueberries
7oz TOBLERONE white chocolate, roughly chopped, 12 triangles reserved for the top

1. Preheat the oven to 400°F.

2. Put the butter and sugar in a medium mixing bowl and beat with an electric whisk until smooth and creamy. Add the beaten egg, a little at a time, beating with every addition.

3. Put the yogurt, vanilla, and milk in a bowl with the flour, baking powder, and baking soda and beat together until smooth and thick. Combine with the butter, sugar, and egg mix.

4. Mix in the blueberries and chopped chocolate with a wooden spoon, then divide the batter evenly between 12 muffin cases. Top each muffin with a piece of chocolate. Bake for 5 minutes, then reduce the temperature to 350°F and bake for a further 25–30 minutes until risen and golden.

5. Let cool on a wire rack. Best enjoyed the day they are baked but will keep in an airtight container for 3–4 days. You can also freeze the muffins individually wrapped in plastic wrap for 1 month. Defrost at room temperature.

SNICKERDOODLE COOKIES

Although the name might suggest this classic has something to do with a chocolate bar of a similar name, these cookies are actually lightly spiced and cake-like in texture. If you don't want to eat them all at once, they can be frozen in a sealed container for up to 1 month.

Makes 16, using 2–3 large baking sheets lined with parchment paper

Prep: 25 minutes
Cook: 10–12 minutes

1⅓ cups (6oz) all-purpose flour
1 teaspoon cream of tartar
½ teaspoon baking soda
1 teaspoon ground cinnamon
3½oz unsalted butter
⅝ cup (4½oz) granulated sugar
1 large egg

1 teaspoon vanilla extract
2¾oz TOBLERONE milk chocolate, roughly chopped
1¾oz TOBLERONE dark chocolate, melted

1. Preheat the oven to 375°F.

2. Sift the flour, cream of tartar, baking soda and cinnamon together in a mixing bowl and set aside.

3. Put the butter and sugar in another bowl and cream together using an electric whisk until smooth and light. Add the egg and vanilla and whisk until fully combined. Stir in the dry ingredients, including the milk chocolate, then use your hands to bring the dough together. Split the mixture into 16 balls. Divide the dough balls between the prepared trays, leaving them room to spread once baked. Lightly flatten each ball with the palm of your hand so it's still quite rounded. Bake for 10 minutes, then let cool.

4. Melt the dark chocolate in a heatproof bowl set over a saucepan of barely simmering water, making sure the bowl doesn't touch the water. Drizzle each cooled cookie with the dark chocolate, then place on a wire rack and let set. These are best eaten on the day they are baked, but will keep for 3–4 days in an airtight container.

CHOCOLATE CHIP COOKIES

Chewy and a little bit crunchy, these freeze well
and if you individually wrap them you can defrost them
one at a time to avoid wasting any.

**Makes 16, using 2–3 large
baking sheets lined with
parchment paper**

Prep: 20 minutes
Cook: 15 minutes

4½oz unsalted butter, softened
⅔ cup (4½oz) soft light brown
sugar
⅝ cup (4½oz) granulated sugar
1 medium egg, beaten
1 teaspoon vanilla extract
1⅜ cup (6½oz) all-purpose flour

½ teaspoon bicarbonate of soda
7oz TOBLERONE milk or fruit and
nut chocolate, half roughly
chopped, half broken into
pieces

1. Preheat the oven to 340°F.

2. Put the butter and sugars in a medium mixing bowl and cream together using an
   electric whisk until light and fluffy. Add the egg and vanilla and beat until combined.
   Use a wooden spoon to stir in the flour, baking soda, the chopped chocolate, and half
   the chunks of chocolate, then bring the dough together with your hands. Divide the
   dough into 16 balls. Divide the dough balls evenly between the lined pans, leaving
   them room to spread once baked. Flatten each cookie a little, then press a piece of
   chocolate into each one. Bake for 13–15 minutes until the cookies are golden around
   the edges.

3. Let cool on a wire rack. Best enjoyed on the day they're baked, but will keep in an
   airtight container for 3–4 days.

CRANBERRY, WHITE TOBLERONE & MACADAMIA COOKIES

Crunchy and buttery, the macadamia nuts and white chocolate in these cookies work perfectly together. They freeze really well and, even better, defrost quickly!

Makes 14, using a 2in cookie cutter and 2-3 baking sheets lined with parchment paper

Prep: 25 minutes
Cook: 22 minutes

5oz unsalted butter
⅓ cup (2¾oz) superfine sugar
1½ cups (7oz) all-purpose flour
2½oz dried cranberries
3½oz TOBLERONE white chocolate, roughly chopped

1¾oz macadamia nuts, roughly chopped

---

1. Put the butter and sugar in a food processor and blitz to form a rough paste. Add the flour and blitz until the dough starts to clump together, then tip into a mixing bowl with the cranberries, chocolate, and macadamia nuts. Gently knead the dough together.

2. Dust the surface with a sprinkle of flour and roll the dough out to 2in thickness with a rolling pin. Use a 2in metal cookie cutter to stamp out 12 cookies and evenly distribute onto the prepared baking sheets. Chill for 1 hour.

3. While the cookies are chilling, preheat the oven to 350°F. Bake for 18-22 minutes until pale golden. Let cool on a wire rack. Best eaten on the day they are made, but will keep for 3-4 days in an airtight container.

Tip: You can freeze the baked biscuits for up to 1 month, just defrost at room temperature.

SALTED CARAMEL & TOBLERONE TRAYBAKE

Soft and buttery sponge swirled with chocolate and caramel.
This cake won't take long to whip up, but no one will ever know!

Makes 16 squares using an 8 x 12in rectangular cake pan lined with parchment paper

Prep: 25 minutes
Cook: 50 minutes

8oz unsalted butter
⅞ cup (7oz) superfine sugar
3 large eggs, beaten
1 teaspoon vanilla extract
5½fl oz sour cream
1⅔ cups (8oz) self-rising flour

¼ teaspoon fine sea salt
5½oz TOBLERONE milk chocolate, roughly chopped
5½oz salted caramel spread

---

1. Preheat the oven to 350°F.

2. Put the butter and sugar in the bowl of a stand mixer and beat until light and fluffy. (You can also do this with an electric whisk.) Pour in the beaten eggs a little at a time, beating after each addition. Add the vanilla, soured cream, flour, salt, and most of the chocolate. Use the stand mixer to slowly combine the batter. Spoon into the prepared tin and dollop the salted caramel over the top. Use a skewer or the end of a spoon to loosely marble the caramel. Bake for 45-50 minutes until risen and golden and a skewer inserted into the center comes out clean.

3. Let cool in the tin, then remove and store in an airtight container. Best eaten on the day it's baked, but will keep for 3-4 days.

Tip: You don't need to swirl the salted caramel sauce through the cake mixture, you can just dollop it on top in small teaspoon-sized balls or even leave it out completely. Try changing the variety of chocolate: this cake works really well with dark or white.

BLACKOUT TOBLERONE CAKE

The ultimate rich chocolate cake.

Serves 12, using 2 x 9in cake pans greased and lined with parchment paper

Prep: 50 minutes
Cook: 30 minutes, plus cooling

10½oz unsalted butter, plus extra for greasing
⅞ cup (3½oz) dark cocoa powder
1⅔ cups (13oz) dark muscovado sugar

1½ tablespoons espresso powder
1⅓ cups (11fl oz) boiling water
7oz TOBLERONE dark chocolate
6 extra large eggs, beaten
1½ tablespoons vanilla extract
2 cups (9oz) all-purpose flour
1½ teaspoons baking soda
1½ teaspoons baking powder
¼ teaspoon fine sea salt
TOBLERONE milk and dark pieces, to decorate

For the icing
10½oz TOBLERONE milk chocolate, roughly chopped
5½oz unsalted butter
2 cups (18fl oz) heavy cream

For the glaze
5½oz TOBLERONE dark chocolate, roughly chopped
2¾oz unsalted butter
5fl oz heavy cream

1. Preheat the oven to 340°F. Put the cocoa, ½ cup of the sugar, and the espresso powder in a large jug, then whisk in the boiling water until smooth. Set aside.

2. Melt the butter and remaining sugar in a large, heavy-based saucepan over a gentle heat, then add the dark chocolate. Stir until melted, then remove from the heat. Add the cocoa-coffee mixture, eggs and vanilla and whisk until smooth.

3. Sift the flour, baking soda, baking powder, and salt together in a large bowl, then slowly whisk into the chocolate mixture. Once smooth, divide evenly between the two prepared pans. Bake for 35-45 minutes or until a skewer comes out cleanly and the cake springs back to the touch. Let cool completely on a wire rack.

4. To make the icing, melt the milk chocolate and butter together in a heatproof bowl set over a saucepan of barely simmering water, making sure the bowl doesn't touch the water. Stir to combine and let cool for 10 minutes. Slowly whisk in the heavy cream until you have a smooth ganache, then cover and chill in the refrigerator for 15 minutes.

5. Slice both cakes in half horizontally, then spread some of the ganache over one cake, top with another layer of cake, cover with ganache, and repeat with the remaining layers. Spread the remaining ganache over the top and sides of the cake. Chill again.

6. To make the glaze, put the dark chocolate in a mixing bowl. Gently melt the butter and cream in a saucepan until steaming. Pour over the chocolate and stir together until the chocolate has melted and you have a thick pourable ganache. Spoon over the cake, letting it drizzle down the sides. Let set at room temperature. Decorate with TOBLERONE chocolate chunks. This will keep in a sealed container for 4-5 days.

MILLIONAIRE'S SHORTBREAD

It's all about the caramel with millionaire's shortbread. Once it has thickened, stop it cooking before it becomes too dark. The caramel will keep bubbling after you remove it from the heat, so take it off just before it changes from a light to a deeper gold. If you can resist it, the shortbread will keep for a week in a sealed container.

Makes 16 squares, using a 9in square cake tin lined with parchment paper

Prep: 30 minutes, plus chilling
Cook: 20 minutes

6oz all-purpose flour
12oz unsalted butter
10oz granulated sugar
8oz light muscovado sugar

1.5 x 13oz can condensed milk
10½oz TOBLERONE milk chocolate

---

1. Preheat the oven to 325°F.

2. To make the shortbread base, put the flour and 4½oz of the butter in a food processor and blitz until it forms breadcrumbs. Add the granulated sugar and blitz until the shortbread begins to clump together. Tip into the lined tin and press into the base so that it forms an even layer. Bake for 25 minutes until pale golden and then let cool in the pan.

3. For the caramel layer, melt the light muscovado sugar and remaining butter in a heavy-based saucepan over a gentle heat. When smooth, stir in the condensed milk, increase the heat and boil for 6-8 minutes, stirring constantly until thickened. The caramel will have turned a pale-medium golden color. Pour onto the cooled shortbread base, then let set in the refrigerator for 3 hours or overnight if possible.

4. Gently melt the chocolate in a small, heatproof bowl set over a saucepan of barely simmering water, making sure the bowl doesn't touch the water. Pour over the set caramel and spread evenly. Return the shortbread to the refrigerator and chill for a further hour or until ready to serve. Slice into 16 squares and keep in an airtight container at room temperature for 3-4 days.

APPLE, CINNAMON, & CHOCOLATE TRAYBAKE

Apple and cinnamon are the perfect combination, and adding white chocolate makes it even better. This cake has a squidgy texture and is lightly spiced. Keep at room temperature in a sealed container for up to 5 days.

Serves 16, using an 8 x 12in cake pan lined with parchment paper

Prep: 30 minutes
Cook: 50 minutes

1lb/approx. 5 cooking apples, such as Bramley
juice of 1 lemon
9oz unsalted butter, softened
1¼ cups (9oz) soft light brown sugar
4 large eggs, beaten

3½fl oz whole milk
1½ teaspoon ground cinnamon
2 cups (9oz) self-rising flour
5½oz TOBLERONE white chocolate, roughly chopped

1. Preheat the oven to 375°F. Peel and thinly slice the apples and squeeze over the lemon juice.

2. Put the butter and sugar in a medium mixing bowl and beat together with an electric whisk until light and fluffy. Slowly add the beaten eggs, a little at a time, whisking between each addition. Add the milk, cinnamon, and flour and slowly beat into the mixture. Use a spatula to fold in half the apples and chocolate. Spoon the batter into the prepared pan and arrange the remaining apples and chocolate on top. Bake for 45-50 minutes until risen and lightly golden.

3. Let cool in the tin for 10 minutes, then remove and let cool completely on a wire rack. Slice into squares and keep in an airtight container in the refrigerator for 1 week.

COCONUT ICE-CREAM CAKE

A giant chocolate cookie cake sandwiched with homemade coconut ice cream. If you're looking for something a little different this is it! It will keep in your freezer for up to 1 month.

Serves 8 generously, using 2 x 8in loose-based cake tins

Prep: 60 minutes
Cook: 25 minutes, plus freezing

7oz unsalted butter, softened
2 cups (9oz) all-purpose flour
¾ cup (1¾oz) dark cocoa powder

1 teaspoon baking powder
½ teaspoon fine sea salt
¾ cup (5½oz) dark brown sugar
¼ cup (1¾oz) granulated sugar
1 large egg, beaten
7oz TOBLERONE dark chocolate, roughly chopped
1¾oz TOBLERONE white chocolate, cut into chunks

For the coconut ice cream
3½oz TOBLERONE white chocolate
13oz can condensed milk
14oz can coconut milk
juice of 1 lime

1. To make the ice cream, gently melt the white chocolate in a small heatproof bowl set over a saucepan of barely simmering water, making sure the bowl doesn't touch the water. Scrape the melted chocolate into a large mixing bowl, then slowly add the condensed milk and beat together using an electric whisk. Add the coconut milk and lime juice and whisk until smooth. Pour into an ice-cream machine, if you have one, and freeze following the machine instructions. Otherwise, freeze in an airtight container for 1 hour, scrape into a food processor and whizz until combined, then freeze for a further 2-3 hours until set but not solid.

2. Meanwhile, preheat the oven to 350°F. Melt the butter in a medium saucepan until it froths and bubbles, then pour into a large mixing bowl and let cool.

3. Sift the flour, cocoa, and baking powder together in another bowl, then mix in the salt using a balloon whisk and set aside. Add the sugars to the cooled melted butter and use a balloon whisk to mix together. Then add the egg, a little at a time, until fully combined. Use a wooden spoon to beat in the flour mixture, then add the dark chocolate. Split the dough in half, then press into the base of the two prepared pans. Top with the white chocolate and bake for 20-25 minutes.

4. Let cool on a wire rack and remove one cookie from its pan. Scoop the coconut ice cream on top of the cookie still in its pan and spread into an even layer. Then sandwich the other cookie on top. Freeze for 3-4 hours or until ready to serve. The cake will keep for 1 month covered in the freezer.

5. Turn the cake out of the pan, cut into wedges, and serve.

3

CELEBRATIONS

CHOCOLATE & GINGER BUNDT CAKE

This chocolate ginger cake is gooey and sticky in the middle and looks fantastic as a centerpiece. If you don't have a Bundt tin, you can bake it in a lined 9in cake pan. It will keep for 4–5 days in a sealed container.

Serves 10–12, using a greased 9in Bundt pan

Prep: 20 minutes
Cook 50 minutes

7oz unsalted butter, plus extra for greasing
⅔ cup (5½oz) superfine sugar

⅔ cup (5½oz) dark muscovado sugar
⅝ cup (7oz) black treacle
2 extra large eggs, beaten
3 pieces of stem ginger in syrup, roughly chopped
1½ cups (7oz) self-rising flour
⅜ cup (1¾oz) cocoa powder
1½ teaspoons ground ginger

⅞ cup (7oz) natural yogurt
3½oz TOBLERONE milk chocolate, chopped, plus extra to decorate

For the topping
cocoa powder, for dusting

1. Preheat the oven to 340°F.

2. Melt the butter, sugars, and treacle in a heavy-based saucepan over a gentle heat, stirring occasionally. Beat the eggs and stem ginger together in a bowl and set aside.

3. In another bowl, sift the flour, cocoa powder, and ground ginger together. Using a balloon whisk, slowly add the melted butter mixture. Then whisk in the egg mixture and yogurt and stir in the chocolate. Pour into the prepared pan and bake for 50 minutes until a skewer inserted into the center comes out clean. Let cool in the pan for 30 minutes, then turn out onto a wire rack to cool completely.

4. Dust with cocoa powder to serve. Store in a sealed container at room temperature for 4–5 days.

TOBLERONE EASTER EGGS

These are the perfect gift for anyone at Easter!

Makes 2 eggs, using 1–2 x 5½in egg molds (two molds is easier as you can make them at the same time)

Prep: 30 minutes, plus chilling

edible gold paint (optional)
10½oz TOBLERONE milk chocolate
2¼oz TOBLERONE white chocolate, to decorate

3½oz mini TOBLERONE chocolate chunks

1. Wash the Easter egg molds thoroughly with hot soapy water, then dry with a clean tea towel. Use cotton wool to buff the inside of the molds – this helps with the shine. If using edible gold paint, gently brush stripes over the insides of the molds.

2. Gently melt 9oz of the milk chocolate in a heatproof bowl set over a saucepan of barely simmering water, making sure the bowl doesn't touch the water. Measure the temperature using a thermometer and let it reach 113°F. As soon as it does, remove the bowl from the heat and add the remaining milk chocolate. Stir with a spatula to melt until it reaches 82°F. This will take a little time. If you are making a dark chocolate egg, take it to 86°F.

3. Meanwhile, melt the white chocolate in a heatproof bowl set over a saucepan of barely simmering water, making sure the bowl doesn't touch the water. Drizzle over the inside of the egg molds, then chill in the refrigerator for 10 minutes to set.

4. As soon as the milk chocolate is at 82°F, pour it into the egg molds (use half the chocolate if you have only one mold). Tip the molds so that the chocolate completely coats all sides and use a brush to help you if necessary. Remove the excess back into the bowl. Scrape a palette knife across the mold to clean the edges. Set the molds flat on a lined baking sheet and chill in the refrigerator for 10 minutes.

5. When the chocolate has set, put on a pair of cotton or plastic gloves, then flex the molds to release the eggs. Preheat the oven to 350°F and put a flat baking sheet in the oven.

6. Fill one mold with the mini TOBLERONE chocolates. Once the tray is hot, remove from the oven. Carefully lift the other chocolate half (wearing the gloves) and put flat side down onto the hot baking sheet. Use a palette knife to help release the eggs if they are struggling to come out. Make sure the chocolate is firm enough before trying to release the eggs. You can then sandwich the two halves together to form an egg. Let set in the refrigerator for 5 minutes. Repeat with the other mold. Wrap and decorate to give as gifts.

EASTER COOKIES

Spiced buttery cookies decorated in Easter colors.
Easter cookie cutters can be bought from online cake
decorating shops or Amazon, or you can design your own.

**Makes 14–16 depending
on your cookie cutters,
using 2 baking sheets lined
with parchment paper**

Prep: 1 hour
Cook: 12–14 minutes

5½oz unsalted butter, softened
⅓ cup (2¾oz) superfine sugar
1 large egg, beaten
1½ cups (7oz) all-purpose flour,
   plus extra for dusting
1 teaspoon ground mixed spice
zest of 1 lemon
3½oz TOBLERONE white
   chocolate, chopped

For the icing
8 cups (2lb) powdered sugar
juice of 2–3 lemons
3–4 different food colorings (we
   used blue, red, and green)

1. Put the butter and sugar in a large mixing bowl and beat with an electric whisk until light and fluffy. Add the egg and whisk until fully combined. Add the flour, mixed spice, and lemon zest and mix with a wooden spoon to form a dough. Then mix in the white chocolate. Shape the dough into a flat disc, wrap in cling film and chill for 1 hour.

2. Sprinkle a little flour over a clean surface, then roll the dough out using a rolling pin to a ¼in thickness. Use the Easter cookie cutters to stamp out the cookies, rerolling the trimmings. Put the cookies onto the prepared baking sheets, leaving 1in between each cookie. Chill for a further 30 minutes and preheat the oven to 350°F. Bake for 12–14 minutes until lightly golden. Cool on the baking sheets for 5 minutes, then move onto a wire rack to cool completely.

3. To make the icing, mix the powdered sugar with the juice of 1–2 lemons, adding the lemon slowly so that you get a thick, pipeable consistency. Add more lemon if it's still too thick. Put one quarter of the icing into a disposable piping bag with a writing nozzle. Squeeze a little more lemon juice into the remaining icing to make it a little looser, then split the icing between three or four different bowls. Add a few drops of your chosen food colorings to the different bowls.

4. Pipe the white icing around the edge of your Easter cookies and decorate with any patterns or shapes you would like. Then use the colored icing to fill the cookies. Let set for 2–3 hours before storing in an airtight container for 2–3 days.

BONKERS BIRTHDAY CAKE

A super fun birthday cake!

Serves 20, using 2 x 8in loose-based cake pans, lined with greaseproof paper and 2 x flat baking sheets lined with parchment paper. You will also need wooden skewers.

Prep: 3–4 hours
Cook: 1 hour 10 minutes, plus chilling

10½oz unsalted butter
⅔ cup (5½oz) superfine sugar
¾ cup (5½oz) light soft brown sugar
6 large eggs
2 cups (9oz) self-rising flour
⅜ cup (1¾oz) dark cocoa powder
3½oz TOBLERONE milk or dark chocolate, grated
3½fl oz whole milk
10½oz TOBLERONE dark chocolate

rainbow sprinkles

For the buttercream
1lb 20oz unsalted butter, softened
8 cups (2lb 4oz) powdered sugar

For the meringues (optional)
2 large egg whites
⅜ cup (4oz) superfine sugar
food coloring pastes

1. Preheat the oven to 350°F. In a stand mixer or with an electric whisk, beat the butter and sugar together until light, creamy, and fluffy. Slowly add the beaten egg, whisking constantly. Pour in the flour, cocoa, chocolate, and milk and mix to a smooth batter. Divide the mixture between the prepared tins and bake for 35–40 minutes until risen and a skewer inserted into the center comes out clean. Let cool for 10 minutes in the pan, then remove and cool on a wire rack.

2. Meanwhile, make the buttercream. If using a stand mixer, add the butter and beat on medium speed for about a minute until smooth. Sift in the icing sugar and mix until thick and smooth. Scrape into a bowl and set aside.

3. Lower the oven to 275°F. Put the egg whites into a medium mixing bowl and whisk until stiff using electric beaters. Then slowly add the sugar, whisking after each spoonful until the sugar dissolves. You will end up with a thick, glossy meringue. Use a small paint brush to paint three different colored stripes in three disposable piping bags, leaving a ½in gap between each stripe. Put one third of the meringue in each piping bag, taking care not to touch the stripes, then snip the end off each. Hold upright, and gently squeeze 1in-wide mini meringues onto the baking sheets with 1in between each. To make lollipops, spiral in a flat round. Bake for 45 minutes, then turn the oven off and let cool with the oven door ajar. Once cool, stick wooden skewers in to make lollipops.

4. Once cooled, halve each cake horizontally. Spread a layer of buttercream evenly on each sponge and top with another cake layer. Repeat with the buttercream and remaining cakes. Cover the whole cake with the remaining buttercream and chill in the refrigerator.

5. To finish, arrange the meringues, rainbow sprinkles and candles or sparklers for the final touches, if you wish! Keep in an airtight container in a cool room for 4–5 days if not eating immediately.

WITCH'S CAT CUPCAKES

Perfect for Halloween parties!
Try changing the color of the fondant to mix them up.

Makes 12, using a 12-hole cupcake pan lined with cases

Prep: 1 hour
Cook: 25 minutes

2 cups (9oz) self-rising flour
⅜ cup (1¾oz) cocoa powder
2 large eggs, beaten
⅜ cup (3½oz) superfine sugar
3½oz TOBLERONE milk
    chocolate, half grated, half
roughly chopped
¾ cup (6fl oz) whole milk
⅓ cup (2¾fl oz) vegetable oil

For the icing
3½oz TOBLERONE dark
    chocolate
7oz unsalted butter, softened
3½ cups (14oz) powdered sugar
3–4 drops of good-quality black
    food coloring (paste works
    best)

To decorate
1¾oz orange or yellow fondant
    icing
8 mini TOBLERONE dark
    chocolate, broken into small
    triangles
1¾oz black fondant icing
4½oz chocolate sticks

1. Preheat the oven to 350°F.

2. Sift the flour and cocoa powder into a mixing bowl. Add the eggs, sugar, grated chocolate, milk, and oil to a jug and whisk together. Slowly whisk the wet ingredients into the dry ones until you have a thick smooth batter. Add in the chopped chocolate. Pour the mix into 12 cupcake cases then bake for 20–25 minutes until risen and a skewer inserted into the centers comes out clean. Let cool on a wire rack.

3. To make the icing, melt the dark chocolate in a small, heatproof bowl set over a saucepan of barely simmering water, making sure the bowl doesn't touch the water. Stir until smooth, then remove from the heat. Meanwhile, in a mixing bowl, beat the butter and powdered sugar together with an electric whisk until smooth. Scrape in the melted chocolate and food coloring, and mix until smooth. Transfer the icing to a large piping bag fitted with a small star nozzle.

4. When the cakes are cool, pipe small stars of icing all over the top of each cupcake. Shape a little of the orange fondant icing into small triangles and stick onto the mini chocolate triangles with black icing – these are the cats' ears. Attach them to the cupcakes with icing. Next, make the eyes. Use the orange fondant as the base and top with a black diamond of fondant. Then stick onto the cupcakes. Shape a nose with an orange triangle of fondant and halve and use the chocolate sticks for whiskers. Keep in an airtight container for 4–5 days in a cool room.

WINTER WONDERLAND CAKE

An indulgent white chocolate delight.

Serves 16, using 3 x 8in cake pans, greased and lined with parchment paper

Prep: 1 hour 10 minutes
Cook: 30 minutes, plus cooling

3½fl oz whole milk
5½oz TOBLERONE white chocolate, roughly chopped

9oz unsalted butter, plus extra for greasing
⅜ cup (3½oz) superfine sugar
150g (5½oz) light soft brown sugar
5 extra large eggs
2 cups (9fl oz) self-rising flour
½ teaspoon ground nutmeg
1 teaspoon ground cinnamon
¼ teaspoon fine sea salt

For the buttercream
⅜ cup (3½fl oz) heavy cream
9oz TOBLERONE white chocolate, roughly chopped, plus extra to decorate
14oz unsalted butter, softened
4 cups (1lb 2oz) icing sugar

1. Preheat the oven to 350°F.

2. Gently melt the milk and white chocolate in a heatproof bowl set over a saucepan of barely simmering water, making sure the bowl doesn't touch the water. Whisk to combine.

3. Put the butter and sugars into the bowl of a stand mixer and beat until light and fluffy. Add the eggs, one at a time, beating constantly. Add the flour and melted chocolate on a low speed. Then add the nutmeg, cinnamon, and salt and combine. Divide the batter equally between the prepared pans and bake for 30 minutes or until a skewer inserted into each center comes out clean. Let cool for 15 minutes, then turn out onto a wire rack to cool completely.

4. To make the icing, gently melt the cream and white chocolate in a heatproof bowl set over a saucepan of barely simmering water, making sure the bowl doesn't touch the water. Stir until smooth and set aside to cool a little.

5. Put the butter and powdered sugar into the bowl of a stand mixer and beat until very smooth. Add the melted chocolate mixture and keep beating. Put two thirds of the buttercream into a large disposable piping bag fitted with a round piping nozzle.

6. Spread one third of the remaining buttercream evenly over the top of each cake using a palette knife, then stack and chill for 30 minutes.

7. Carefully pipe buttercream around the cake, piping one full ring at a time. Once you are halfway up the cake, use a palette knife to smooth the buttercream perfectly around the edges. Then squeeze a little more icing on top and smooth that. Pipe small blobs in concentric circles around the top of the cake. Decorate the top with varying sizes of TOBLERONE white chocolate chunks to mimic mountains. Keep in a sealed container in the refrigerator for 4-5 days. Bring to room temperature 2 hours before serving.

GORNERGRAT EXPRESS!

The Gornergrat is Europe's highest railway linking Zermatt, situated at 5.262ft above sea level, to the summit of Gornergrat at 10,135ft. Along the way it affords you panoramic views of the Matterhorn, the mountain that features as the TOBLERONE logo. This cake is a bit of fun, perfect for any celebration! If you prefer, you can make it your own with different colors and designs.

Serves 25, using a 10in springform cake tin and 2 x 6in cake pans, greased and lined with parchment paper

Prep: 3 hours
Cook: 1 hour 10 minutes, plus chilling

7oz TOBLERONE dark chocolate
1lb unsalted butter, softened, plus extra for greasing
2 cups (1lb) golden superfine sugar

8 extra large eggs, beaten
3½ cups (1lb) self-rising flour
⅜ cup (1¾oz) cocoa powder

For the buttercream
12oz unsalted butter, softened
6 cups (1lb 9oz) powdered sugar, plus extra to decorate

For the royal icing
3 large egg whites
4¼ cups (1lb 5oz) icing sugar
juice of 1 lemon

To decorate
black, red, and green food coloring
3½oz black fondant icing
4½oz chocolate sticks, such as Matchmakers
1 ready-made chocolate Swiss roll, approx 8in in length
1 large triangle of TOBLERONE dark chocolate
10 mini TOBLERONE milk chocolates

1. Preheat the oven to 350°F.

2. Melt the dark chocolate in a heatproof bowl set over a saucepan of barely simmering water, making sure the bowl doesn't touch the water. Stir until smooth and set aside.

3. Put the butter and sugar in the bowl of a stand mixer and beat on high speed until light and fluffy. (You can also do this with an electric whisk, but there is a lot of cake batter to contend with.) Keep the mixer going on a steady speed and slowly add the eggs, fully combining before adding more. Add the flour, cocoa, and melted chocolate and mix together on a low speed. Pour the mixture into the two small cake tins, leaving ½in around the top. Then pour the remaining batter into the 10in cake tin. Bake for 30 minutes, then check the small cakes. If cooked, remove from the oven and continue baking the large cake for a further 40–45 minutes until a skewer inserted into the center comes out clean. If the small cakes are still a little soft after 30 minutes, bake for a further 5–10 minutes. This is the same for the large cake.

4. Leave all the cakes to cool for 10–15 minutes, then remove from the pans and cool completely on a wire rack. Meanwhile, make the buttercream. Put the butter and half the powdered sugar in the bowl of a stand mixer and beat together until creamy. Wrap a tea towel over the stand mixer to prevent the powdered sugar from going everywhere. Add the remaining powdered sugar and beat again until very smooth. Reserve a quarter of the buttercream in another bowl, cover both bowls with plastic wrap and set aside.

5. When the cakes are cool, slice the large cake in half horizontally with a bread knife to make two even-sized cakes. Then halve the two smaller cakes vertically so you have four semicircles. Chill all the cakes in the freezer for 15 minutes; this makes them easier to ice.

6. Spread the buttercream over the two large halved cakes and top with each other. Spread the buttercream all over the cake as smoothly as possible. Add one semicircle of small cake on top in the middle at the back edge of the cake. Spread the buttercream over this, then layer up two more semicircles, leaving you with one left over for the trees. Chill in the refrigerator for 30 minutes.

7. Meanwhile, make the royal icing. Clean the stand mixer out again and add the egg whites. Use the whisk attachment to mix until they form medium peaks. Add the powdered sugar, wrapping a tea towel over the mixer to stop it going everywhere. Mix until thick, shiny, and smooth, then add the lemon juice and whisk again.

8. Put half the reserved buttercream in a mixing bowl with some green food coloring and mix until smooth. Add the food coloring slowly to make sure you get the color you want. Transfer this to a disposable piping bag with a small star nozzle. Color the remaining buttercream in black, apart from 1 tablespoon in red for the light (optional) for the train. Transfer the black buttercream into a disposable piping bag. You can also do this with the red or use a small teaspoon to dollop on the sugar for the light.

9. Cover the cake with the royal icing, using a palette knife to spread the icing smoothly. You can keep it very smooth or make it a little uneven as if it were piles of snow. Roll out the black fondant icing using a little icing sugar to form a rough oval. This is the tunnel opening. Use a sharp knife to cut out a neater oval, keeping the bottom edge straight so it will sit neatly on the cake. Stick it in on the end of the cake tunnel to form the opening.

10. Use the chocolate sticks to make a train track in front of the tunnel (reserving two chocolate sticks to make a sign later, if you wish). Now, make the train. Slice off one-third of the Swiss roll and sit upright against the tunnel – this is the cab part of the train. Pipe a little black buttercream on the side and press the larger piece of Swiss roll flat against it to make the front of the train, sitting on the tracks – it should look a little like an 'L' on its back. Pipe black buttercream in small star shapes neatly over the Swiss roll train, in your preferred pattern. Put a little buttercream on top of the cab part and stick on the large piece of dark chocolate. Use the black buttercream to fill in wheels and lights on the train – plus any other details you would like to draw. You can dollop on the red buttercream for the light if you wish.

11. Each mini TOBLERONE chocolate has three triangles, break off each of these triangles and use them to decorate around the black fondant tunnel entrance. Slice the remaining semicircle of cake into small cone shapes for trees using a small serrated knife. Pipe the green buttercream around each tree and place on the cake. If you want to make a sign, heat a metal knife using a gas flame from the hob or a chef's blow torch and use it to melt one end of a chocolate stick. Break another chocolate stick in half to make a cross. Melt a little chocolate on one of them so you can stick them together in the centre. Then stick the cross to the melted end of the other chocolate stick and leave to set in the refrigerator. Once firm, stick into the cake. Use your imagination to add as many features as you like. Finish the cake with a dusting of icing sugar to look like snow! Best eaten in 3–4 days. Store in the refrigerator, loosely covered with cling film. Bring up to room temperature 1–2 hours before serving.

4

DESSERTS

CHOCOLATE MUG CAKE

This is the fastest way to TOBLERONE chocolate cake! Perfect for nights when you're home alone and need something sweet or a special treat. Once you have the formula, it's so easy to swap out different flavors. Try removing the cocoa powder and popping in raspberries. Swap dark chocolate for white and add blueberries or stir in mashed banana.

Makes 1, using a 12–14fl oz mug

Prep: 10 minutes
Cook: 1–2 minutes

3 tablespoons superfine sugar
5 tablespoons all-purpose flour
½ teaspoon baking powder
2 tablespoons cocoa powder
pinch of fine sea salt
1 tablespoon whole milk

2 tablespoons vegetable oil
1 large egg, beaten
1oz TOBLERONE milk chocolate, roughly chopped
heavy or half-and-half cream, to serve

1. Put the sugar, flour, baking powder, cocoa, and salt in a mixing bowl and stir together with a balloon whisk. Add the milk, oil, and egg and whisk to a smooth batter. Stir in most of the chocolate and spoon into your mug.

2. Sprinkle over the remaining chocolate. Cook for 1 minute 40 seconds for a 600W microwave. For an 800W microwave, reduce the cooking time by 20 seconds. Let stand for 1 minute, then enjoy with a drizzle of cream.

MINT CHOC ICE-CREAM ROLL

Mint Choc Chip is an ice cream classic and works perfectly
with chocolate Swiss roll. A winner with children and adults alike,
it looks fantastic, though requires a bit of time to make.
It will keep in the freezer for 1-2 months.

**Serves 8-10, using a 8 x 12in
Swiss roll pan lined with
parchment paper**

**Prep: 2 hours
Cook: 15 minutes, plus freezing**

For the ice cream
5 large egg yolks
⅓ cup (2¾oz) superfine sugar
15fl oz (16fl oz) heavy cream

⅝ cup (5fl oz) whole milk
1 vanilla bean, split
1 teaspoon peppermint extract
3-4 drops of green food coloring
100g (3½oz) TOBLERONE milk or
  coconut chocolate, roughly
  chopped

For the cake
4 large eggs
½ cup (4½oz) superfine sugar,

plus extra for dusting
⅝ cup (2¾oz) all-purpose flour
¼ cup (1oz) cocoa powder
1 teaspoon baking powder

To decorate
2¼oz TOBLERONE white
  chocolate
1½oz TOBLERONE milk
  chocolate, roughly chopped

1. To make the ice cream, mix the egg yolks and sugar together in a medium bowl. Gently
   heat the cream, milk, and split vanilla bean in a heavy-based saucepan. Once steaming,
   use a balloon whisk to mix the cream mixture into the egg yolks. Pour the custard back
   into the saucepan, whisking constantly, and heat gently for 8-10 minutes until
   thickened and simmering. When it coats the back of a wooden spoon, pour into a
   clean bowl and add the peppermint extract and food coloring. Let cool completely.

2. Pour the cooled custard into an ice-cream machine, if you have one, and freeze
   following the machine instructions, then stir in the chocolate chunks after churning.
   If you don't have a machine, pour the custard into an airtight container, freeze for
   1 hour, then whisk and stir in the chocolate. Freeze for about 2 hours until nearly
   frozen, or for 30 minutes if using a machine.

3. Meanwhile, preheat the oven to 350°F.

4. To make the cake, put the eggs and sugar in a mixing bowl and beat with an electric
   whisk for 5 minutes until the mixture is pale and mousse-like. Sift in the flour, cocoa,
   and baking powder and use a large metal spoon to gently fold together. Spread evenly
   in the prepared pan and bake for 12-15 minutes until it has risen and springs back to
   the touch. Let cool for 5 minutes.

5. Put a sheet of parchment paper larger than the cake on a clean surface and dust with superfine sugar. Turn the cake out of the pan onto the paper and carefully peel off the paper on the bottom of the cake. Use the parchment paper to gently roll the long edge of the cake up and leave to cool completely.

6. Once the ice cream has nearly frozen, cut a piece of parchment paper slightly longer than the length of the rolled cake. Spoon the ice cream along the length, then roll the paper as tight as you can to shape the ice cream into a cylinder about 12in long. Once smooth, refreeze for 1–2 hours until completely solid.

7. When the cake and ice cream are both cool, unroll the cake and unwrap the ice cream. Sit the frozen cylinder of ice cream along the length of the cake and roll the cake tightly around the ice cream. Wrap tightly in a piece of parchment paper and return to the freezer for at least 2 hours or until you are ready to serve.

8. To serve, melt the white chocolate in a small, heatproof bowl set over a saucepan of barely simmering water, making sure the bowl doesn't touch the water. Drizzle over the cake. Sprinkle over the roughly chopped milk chocolate and decorate with small pieces of chocolate if you wish. Slice into 1in thick slices to serve. Wrap in a double layer of plastic wrap and keep in the freezer for up to 1 month.

TOBLERONE MOUSSE
WITH ALMOND BRITTLE

The perfect contrast of light and airy chocolate mousse
and crunchy brittle. The mousse will keep in the refrigerator
for 3-4 days, though the brittle will soften, so make it
on the day you intend to eat them.

**Serves 6, using 6 x 5fl oz
ramekins or a 1¼-pint dish**

**Prep: 40 minutes, plus
minimum 2 hours chilling**

5½oz TOBLERONE milk chocolate
2 extra large eggs, separated
7fl oz heavy cream
1 tablespoon cocoa powder

For the brittle
2¾oz almonds, lightly toasted
and roughly chopped
⅜ cup (3½oz) superfine sugar

---

1. Melt the chocolate in a heatproof bowl set over a saucepan of barely simmering water, making sure the bowl doesn't touch the water. Let cool for 5 minutes.

2. Beat the egg whites with an electric whisk until they form medium peaks – they want to hold their shape but not be stiff. In another bowl, whisk the heavy cream until it forms medium peaks.

3. Beat the egg yolks and cocoa powder into the melted chocolate, then fold the cream in first. Once fully combined, fold in the egg whites and divide between the ramekins or pour into the large dish. Cover with plastic wrap and chill for at least 2 hours or up to 2 days.

4. An hour before you want to serve the mousse, put a piece of parchment paper on a baking sheet and sprinkle over half the almonds. Put the sugar and 2fl oz water in a non-stick frying pan. Simmer over medium heat and swirl the pan to dissolve the sugar. Once dissolved, leave to simmer. When it starts to turn golden, swirl the pan to mix the caramel. This should take 4-5 minutes. Once the caramel is a deep golden, pour over the chopped almonds. Tilt the tray to spread the caramel, then scatter over the remaining chopped almonds. Let cool completely.

5. When the brittle is cold and solid, move onto a cutting board and roughly chop and break into small pieces. Serve the mousse with a scattering of caramel.

AMARETTI, ORANGE, & TOBLERONE LAYERED DESSERTS

Speedy and impressive, these are perfect for when you want to make something in advance. Try swapping the Amaretto for whatever you have left over in your cupboard!

Makes 4 large or 8 small desserts, using 4 x 10fl oz glasses or 8 x 3½–5fl oz glasses or dessert bowls

Prep: 30 minutes, plus chilling

2 gelatin leaves
3½oz amaretti cookies, roughly chopped
5 teaspoons Amaretto
3½oz TOBLERONE milk chocolate
4 oranges, sliced into segments and all pith and peel removed, plus zest of 2

1⅔ cups (14fl oz) good-quality ready-made custard
⅝ cup (5fl oz) heavy cream
1 tablespoon powdered sugar
4-8 mini TOBLERONE chocolates, to decorate

1. Put the gelatin leaves in a bowl and cover with cold water. Leave to soften for 5 minutes. Meanwhile, divide two thirds of the amaretti between the glasses, making them as flat as possible. Pour ½ teaspoon of Amaretto over each glass, or ¼ teaspoon if using eight glasses, then set aside.

2. Melt the chocolate in a heatproof bowl set over a saucepan of barely simmering water, making sure the bowl doesn't touch the water. Remove from the heat and set aside for a few minutes.

3. In a small bowl, mix the orange zest, 1 tablespoon of orange juice (use the peel to squeeze the juice), the remaining Amaretto, and the custard together. Add the melted chocolate and whisk until smooth. Spoon one third of the chocolate custard into a saucepan and warm over a gentle heat. Squeeze out the excess water from the gelatin and add to the pan. Stir continuously until the gelatin melts – don't let it boil. Now stir the warm mixture back into the chocolate custard until smooth. Let cool in the refrigerator, covered with plastic wrap, for 10 minutes.

4. Meanwhile, layer the orange segments on top of the amaretti in the glasses. Carefully pour about ½in of the chocolate custard over the oranges, pouring in the center so it doesn't pool over the oranges. Chill in the refrigerator for 15 minutes, then top with the remaining custard. Chill for 1 hour or until set.

5. Whip the cream and powdered sugar together. Dollop the cream on top of the desserts, sprinkle over the remaining amaretti and top with a mini TOBLERONE chocolate. Chill until ready to eat. These will keep for 2 days, covered with plastic wrap, in the refrigerator.

CHOCOLATE FONDANTS

These desserts have gooey melted white chocolate in the center that swirls with the dark chocolate cake. If white chocolate isn't your favorite, swap the center chocolate piece for dark or milk.

Serves 6, using 6 dariole molds or ramekins

Prep: 30 minutes
Cook: 12 minutes, plus chilling

7oz unsalted butter, 1½oz melted, for brushing, and 5¾oz diced into small cubes
cocoa powder, for dusting
5¾oz TOBLERONE dark chocolate
3 large eggs and 3 yolks

⅔ cup (5¾oz) superfine sugar
1¼ cup (5¾oz) all-purpose flour
6 TOBLERONE white chocolate triangles from a 7oz bar
ice cream or heavy cream, to serve

1. First, prepare the molds. Generously brush each mold with the melted butter and then freeze for 10 minutes. Brush with more butter then dust with cocoa powder and keep in the freezer until ready to use.

2. Gently melt the chocolate and diced butter in a heatproof bowl set over a saucepan of barely simmering water, making sure the bowl doesn't touch the water. Stir until smooth, then leave to cool for 10 minutes.

3. In a separate bowl, beat the eggs, yolks, and sugar together with an electric whisk for 3–4 minutes until pale and thickened – you should be able to leave a trail in the mix. Add the melted chocolate and flour and gently fold into the eggs. Pour into a jug and fill each mold halfway. Put a piece of chocolate on its side into each mold, then pour over more batter covering the chocolate. Chill in the refrigerator for 30 minutes or up to 24 hours.

4. Preheat the oven to 400°F.

5. Put the fondants on a baking sheet and bake for 12 minutes until the tops have formed a crust and the sides have started to come away from the edges. Remove from the oven and let cool for a minute.

6. Turn the fondants out onto dessert plates and serve with ice cream or heavy cream.

Tip: You can freeze the fondants for up to 1 month. Cook from frozen, adding 5 minutes to cooking time.

THREE-INGREDIENT
CHOCOLATE TORTE

This torte is light and mousse-like in texture.
It's simple to make and only uses three ingredients! The torte
will keep for 2-3 days in a sealed container in the refrigerator.

Serves 8-10, using an 8in loose-bottomed tin, greased and lined with greaseproof paper

Prep: 20 minutes
Cook: 25 minutes

7oz unsalted butter, plus extra for greasing
10½oz TOBLERONE dark chocolate, plus extra for decorating

6 large eggs, separated, yolks beaten
berries and whipped cream, to serve (optional)

1. Preheat the oven to 340°F.

2. Melt the butter and chocolate in a medium saucepan over a gentle heat. Stir with a wooden spoon until smooth, then pour into a mixing bowl and let cool for 5 minutes.

3. Put the egg whites in a clean mixing bowl and beat with an electric whisk until they form medium peaks. Add the beaten egg yolks to the melted chocolate mixture and stir together. Use a large metal spoon to fold the egg whites into the cake batter, being careful not to knock the air out of the mixture. Pour the batter into the prepared pan and bake for 25 minutes until risen and a little firm and cracked – this is normal! Let cool in the tin.

4. To serve, remove the torte from the pan and grate over some more chocolate. Serve with berries and whipped cream, if you like. Store in a sealed container in the refrigerator for 2-3 days.

BAKED CHOCOLATE CHEESECAKE

Not only is this dessert a velvety and rich showstopper
but also – even better – you can make it in advance.

Serves 14, using a 9in springform pan lined with parchment paper taller than the pan and greased well

Prep: 40 minutes
Cook: 1 hour 20 minutes

10½oz OREO cookies
2¼oz salted butter, plus extra for greasing
7oz TOBLERONE dark chocolate, plus extra to decorate
1lb 2oz full-fat cream cheese
9oz mascarpone
3½fl oz heavy cream
1 cup (8oz) superfine sugar
5 large eggs
cherries, to decorate

For the icing
3½fl oz heavy cream
7oz cream cheese
⅜ cup (1¾oz) powdered sugar

1. Preheat the oven to 325°F.

2. Put the cookies in a sealable food bag and bash into crumbs or blitz in a food processor if you have one. Melt the butter in a saucepan over medium heat, then stir in the cookies. Mix well, then press into the prepared pan. Chill in the refrigerator for 20 minutes.

3. Meanwhile, melt the chocolate in a heatproof bowl set over a saucepan of barely simmering water, making sure the bowl doesn't touch the water. Stir until smooth, then set aside.

4. Beat the cream cheese, mascarpone and heavy cream together with an electric whisk until smooth. Add the sugar and eggs, beat again, then add the melted chocolate and mix until smooth. Pour over the base, ensuring the top is smooth. Wrap the outside of the pan in parchment paper, then in two layers of foil, making sure the cake pan is fully sealed. Sit in a roasting tray larger than the tin. Pour warm water around the pan until it comes halfway up the sides, then place in the center of the oven. Bake for 1 hour 20 minutes until set but with a good wobble.

5. Run a small, flat palette knife around the edge of the cheesecake – this will help prevent cracks when it cools - and let cool.

6. Put the icing ingredients in a mixing bowl and beat with an electric whisk until smooth. Carefully unclip the pan and transfer the cheesecake to a serving plate. Dollop the icing onto the center of the cooled cheesecake and top with cherries and chocolate chunks. Keep in the refrigerator until ready to serve. Any leftovers will keep in the refrigerator for 2-3 days.

MILK TOBLERONE, ALMOND, & PEAR PIE

Chocolate, pear, and almond are another classic combination.
This pie not only looks amazing but tastes it too.

**Serves 8–10, using a
9in fluted pie tin**

**Prep: 50 minutes
Cook: 1 hour 10 minutes,
plus chilling**

For the pastry
4½oz unsalted butter, chilled

2 cups (9oz) all-purpose flour
pinch of fine sea salt
1 large egg yolk
2–3 tablespoons cold water

For the filling
3½oz TOBLERONE milk chocolate
3½oz unsalted butter
⅜ cup (3½oz) superfine sugar

2 large eggs
3½oz ground almonds
½ teaspoon almond extract
2 tablespoons all-purpose flour
1 tablespoon dark cocoa powder
2 ripe blush pears, peeled, cored
   and sliced into 8 pieces

crème fraîche or ice cream, to serve

1. To make the pastry, put the butter, flour, and salt in a food processor and pulse to a breadcrumb texture. Add the egg yolk and 2 tablespoons of the water and pulse. The pastry should start to come together but may need a teaspoon more water. Be careful not to over-blend as this will make the pastry tough. Shape into a flat disc, cover in plastic wrap and chill in the freezer for 10 minutes.

2. Dust a clean surface with flour, then roll the pastry out to ⅛in thickness so that there is enough pastry to line the tin. Lift over the tin, then lower and carefully press into the base and sides of the tin. Trim any excess, then return to the freezer for 20 minutes.

3. Meanwhile, preheat the oven to 425°F. Line the pastry shell with parchment paper or foil, fill with baking beans and bake for 20 minutes. Remove the beans and bake for a further 3 minutes until sandy on the bottom of the pastry. Leave to cool and reduce the oven temperature to 375°F.

4. Gently melt the chocolate in a heatproof bowl set over a saucepan of barely simmering water, making sure the bowl doesn't touch the water. Stir until smooth, then set aside.

5. To make the filling, put the butter and sugar in a large mixing bowl and beat with an electric whisk until light and fluffy. Slowly add the eggs, whisking between each addition. Stir in the ground almonds, almond extract, flour, and cocoa powder. Stir in the melted chocolate, then spoon the filling into the cooked pastry case.

6. Arrange the pears on top of the filling and bake for 40–45 minutes until the frangipane has set and the pears are tender. Let cool a little before slicing or chill completely and enjoy cold with a dollop of crème frâiche. Store in the refrigerator in an airtight container for 2–3 days.

COFFEE TRAYBAKE

A real crowd-pleaser and sophisticated treat.

Serves 20, using an 8 x 12in non-stick cake tin lined with greaseproof paper, greased with vegetable oil, and an approx. 12 x 16in cake board

Prep: 1 hour 30 minutes
Cook: 50 minutes

7fl oz vegetable oil, plus extra
2⅛ cups (9¾oz) all-purpose flour
3½oz cocoa powder
2 teaspoons baking powder
1 teaspoon baking soda
1½ cups (12oz) superfine sugar
1 cup (9½fl oz) buttermilk
⅔ cup (5½fl oz) strong coffee
1 tablespoon vanilla extract

3 large eggs, beaten
3½oz TOBLERONE milk chocolate, roughly chopped, plus extra left whole

For the ganache
3½fl oz heavy cream
3½oz TOBLERONE dark chocolate, roughly chopped

1. Preheat the oven to 350°F.

2. Mix the flour, cocoa, baking powder, and baking soda together in a large bowl. Combine the sugar, buttermilk, coffee, and vanilla in a large jug. Add the eggs and whisk until smooth. Pour the wet ingredients into the dry ones and use a balloon whisk to beat until smooth. Pour into the prepared tin and sprinkle over the chopped chocolate. Bake for 45–50 minutes until a skewer inserted into the center comes out clean. Bake for a further for 5 minutes if necessary. Leave to cool in the pan for 15 minutes, then turn out onto a wire rack to cool completely.

3. To make the ganache, pour the cream into a small saucepan and gently heat until steaming. Put the dark chocolate in a bowl and pour over the hot cream. Use a spatula to stir the cream into the chocolate and let it melt. Keep stirring until thick and smooth. Chill in the refrigerator for 20 minutes to firm up, then transfer to a disposable piping bag fitted with a rose petal or star nozzle.

4. Remove the cake from its tin and sit on a cake board; if it's moving a little, secure with some ganache. Pipe a little icing on the bottom of each chocolate triangle and place them on the cake in a decorative manner. You can place randomly or create a pattern.

Tip: You can freeze the uniced sponge for up to 1 month. Fully defrost, then ice.